Places We Share

By Sally Hewitt
Photographs by Chris Fairclough

W
FRANKLIN WATTS
LONDON·SYDNEY

This edition 2004

Franklin Watts
96 Leonard Street
London EC2A 4XD

Franklin Watts Australia
45-51 Huntley Street
Alexandria
NSW 2015

Editor: Samantha Armstrong
Consultant: Steven Watts, School of Education, University of Sunderland
Designer: Louise Snowdon
Photographs: Chris Fairclough

A CIP catalogue record for this book is
available from the British Library
Dewey Decimal Classification Number: 725

ISBN 0 7496 5204 7

Printed in Malaysia

Contents

Places we share

There are lots of places that we all share.
In the middle of a busy town, there are squares and
parks where people can rest, read or chat to each other.

- Look at the picture above. Why do you think the people
have stopped here?
- What makes this a pleasant place to sit?
- Would you sit here if the weather was cold or wet?
- Where could you sit instead?

The places we share are used for different things. Some public places have rules that make sure everyone can enjoy themselves.

• Why do you think skateboarding and rollerskating are not allowed in this place?

The sound of running water in the fountain reminds visitors of the countryside.

• What else do you think you could hear in this square?

A cleaner sweeps up the rubbish.

• How could you help to keep the square clean?

The village hall

Villages often have a hall where local people
get together for meetings, parties and for all kinds
of other activities.

- What event is taking place in this village hall?
- The outside of the hall has been decorated for the fete.
What do you think the inside of the hall looks like?

Leaflets on the notice board tell people about events in the village.

- The notice board is outside the hall. Is this a good place for it? Why?
- If you lived here, how would you use the hall?

This village has won two prizes.

- What are they for?
- Why are the shields on the village hall wall and not in someone's house?

The town hall

This town hall looks very important. The local council works in the town hall. The local council deals with houses, schools and all the streets in the area.

- What do you think makes the town hall look so important?
- What other things might the local council deal with?

10

You have to walk under a grand arch and up some steps to get to the entrance.

• Do you think this doorway helps visitors to feel welcome?

The clock tower rises high above the rest of the building.

• Why do you think the clock tower is so tall?

The town hall was built over 100 years ago.

BUILDING OF ARCHITECTURAL OR HISTORIC INTEREST
GRADE 1
TOWN HALL (1877)
VICTORIAN GOTHIC STYLE
ARCHITECT—ALFRED WATERHOUSE
(1830-1905)

• What do you think it would look like if it had been built today?

11

Using the library

Everyone can go to the library. It is a place to sit quietly and read, to find out things you want to know, to use the Internet and to borrow books, videos, CDs and tapes.

- What are the different people doing in this library?
- What do you think it sounds like here?
- If you needed some help, what would you do?

Children can enjoy books in their own part of the library.

- Why do you think some of the children's books are in boxes and not on shelves?
- Would you like to visit this library?
- What would you do there?

Visiting a museum

The children and adults in this photograph are all enjoying a day out at a motor museum. There are lots of things to see and do indoors, and outdoors.

- Is a motor museum a good place to find out about travel?
- Look at the sign in the photograph. Which part of the museum would you like to visit?

The cars on display inside the museum are valuable. They need to be sheltered from the weather.

- Do you think this building was built to be a museum?
- How can you tell?

The boys are learning how an engine works by trying it out for themselves.

- What else might you be able to learn about at a motor museum?

In the park

A park is an open space of grass, trees and flowers in a town, a city or near to where people live. A park often has a pond or a playground, like the one in these pictures.

• Why do you think a city is a good place to have a park?

There is space for a big climbing frame, swings and a see-saw.

- What do you do when you visit your local park?
- How is playing in a park playground different from playing in a garden?
- What equipment is best in a park playground?

A fence and a soft covering on the ground help to keep the children safe.

- How do the fence and the soft ground protect the children?
- What other things can you see that are there for safety?

At the swimming pool

Swimming pools are for everyone to enjoy. Babies and children splash about and have fun in the shallow paddling pool, while their parents keep a careful watch.

- What different things can you see that are there to keep the children safe?
- What makes the pool seem bright and friendly?

Good swimmers swim fast up and down the main pool to keep fit and to train for racing.

• Can you see how they manage not to bump into each other?

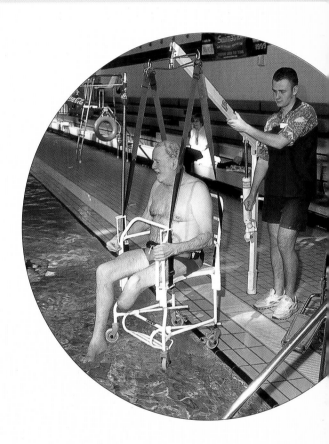

Staff help everyone to enjoy the pools. This man is being lowered into the water in a chair.

Little children learn to swim in deep water.

• Why do you think you have a shower when you go into the pool and another when you come out?
• What do you think you would hear and smell at the swimming pool?

Places to eat

It's a treat to go to a restaurant. This family order food to take away. The restaurant is busy. Children at a birthday party enjoy their food.

• How do you know what food to choose?
• Would you like to have a party in a restaurant? Why?

Some restaurants have tables outside. A waitress takes your order and returns with the food you have chosen.

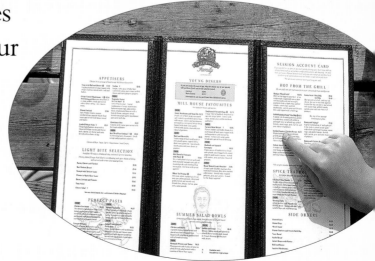

- Do you think it is fun to eat outside? Why?
- What information can you find on a menu?

Going to the cinema

A cinema complex has several screens showing different films. Some are children's films and others are for adults.

- What can you buy to eat and drink while you are watching the film?

No one can get in to watch a film without a ticket.

- Why does the ticket have the date, a seat number and the time of the film printed on it?

Posters often advertise other films that are on at the cinema, or films that are coming soon.

Places to worship

People of the same religion get together regularly to worship. They meet in each other's houses, halls, churches, chapels, mosques, synagogues, gurdwaras, mandirs or temples.

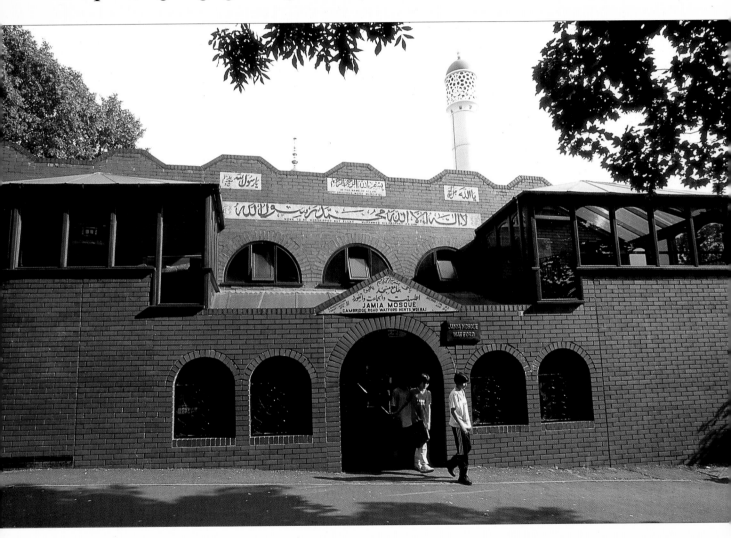

This is a mosque. Five times a day, a crier calls Muslims to prayer from the tall tower called a minaret.

• What places of worship are in your neighbourhood?

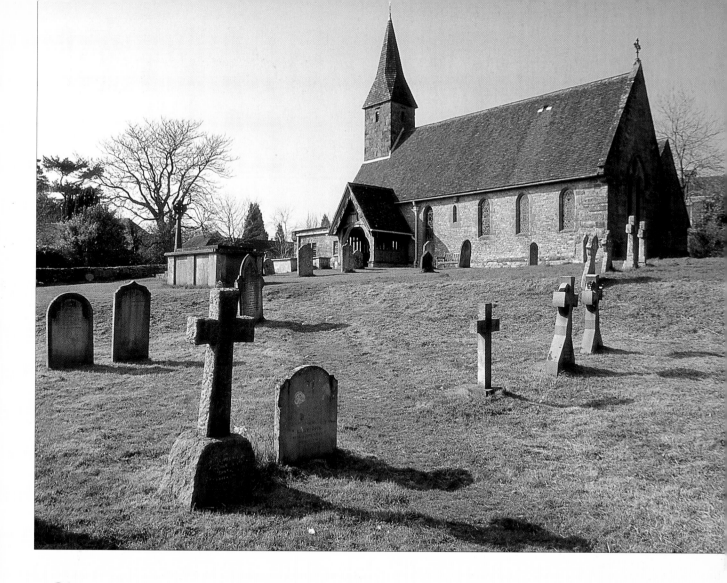

Christians have worshipped in this old church for hundreds of years. There are services every Sunday. People also go to church for weddings and funerals.

- Is there a church near where you live?
- Is it like this church? How is it different?

Bells peal out from the tower to call people to church.

- Have you heard church bells? Can you describe how they sound?

Going to hospital

We go to hospital when we get hurt, or if we are ill or need an operation. The doctors and nurses who work there take care of us.

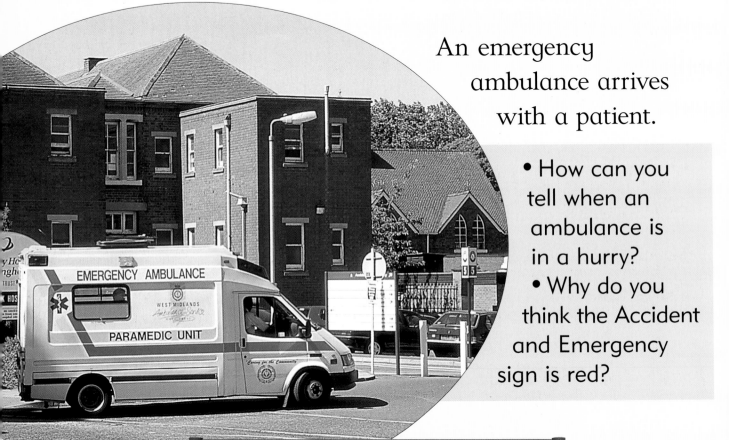

An emergency ambulance arrives with a patient.

- How can you tell when an ambulance is in a hurry?
- Why do you think the Accident and Emergency sign is red?

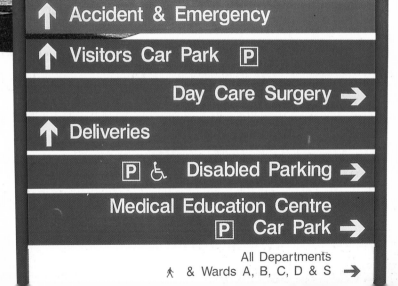

↑	Accident & Emergency
↑	Visitors Car Park P
	Day Care Surgery →
↑	Deliveries
	P & Disabled Parking →
	Medical Education Centre P Car Park →
	All Departments
	⚇ & Wards A, B, C, D & S →

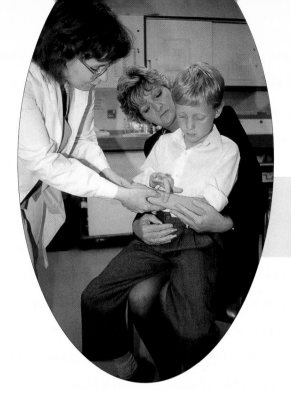

In the Accident and Emergency unit, a doctor checks the boy's hurt arm.

• Why do you think his mother is with him?

This is not an emergency ambulance.

• What kind of patients do you think it brings to the hospital?

This patient is staying overnight in the hospital. The nurse looks after her.

• Have you been to hospital?
• What would you tell your friends about your visit?

Key words

Borrow   you can borrow books, videos, tapes and CDs for a short time from a library. The library keeps a record of what you borrow and stamps it with a date that tells you when you must bring it back.

Emergency   an emergency is a dangerous situation that needs attention as quickly as possible. Emergency ambulances take people to hospital if they are very ill or have had a bad accident.

Events   an event is a special occasion like a fair, a sports day or dance. A village hall is often used for events.

Local   local is everything nearby in your neighbourhood.

Local council   a local council is a group of people who work in the town hall. They look after schools, houses and streets in the local area.

Menu   at a restaurant, a menu tells you what you can buy to eat and drink and how much it costs.

Museum   a museum is a place where a collection of interesting things is put on display for people to look at and learn about.

Park   a park is where people can go to play sport and enjoy grass, trees, flowers, lakes and ponds.

Restaurant   a restaurant is a place where you can buy a meal. You might eat your meal at the restaurant, or take it away to eat at home.

Rules   rules tell you how to behave and what is or is not allowed. They help everyone to be safe and happy.

Square   a square is a peaceful space in the middle of a busy town where traffic is not allowed.

Ticket   a ticket shows that you have paid to get into places like museums and cinemas. You need a ticket to ride on a bus or a train.

Think about places for everyone

1. Is there a park or a garden near where you live?

- What different ways do people use it?
- What do you do when you go there?

2. Choose a place we share from this book and plan a birthday party there.

- What kinds of things would you do with your friends?
- Where would you have your birthday meal?
- Are all the places in this book good for a party?

3. Find out about the places to share near where you live.

- Which ones have you visited?
- Which ones would you like to visit?

4. Choose a place you have visited.

- Tell a friend what you enjoyed about it.
- Tell them what you didn't enjoy.

5. Imagine you owned a museum and draw a plan of it.

- What kind of museum would it be?
- Would it be indoors, outdoors or both?
- What special attractions would you put on?

Index